THE

DIVINE ARCHER

THE DIVINE ARCHER

FOUNDED ON THE INDIAN EPIC OF THE RAMAYANA WITH TWO STORIES FROM THE MAHABHARATA

F. J. GOULD

GYAN

Published by

Gyan Publishing House
5, Ansari Road
Daryaganj, New Delhi-110002
Phone: 011-47034999, 9811692060
E-mail: books@gyanbooks.com

Distribution Network
gyanbooks.com
India, USA, Canada, UK, Australia, France

ISBN : 978-81-212-9228-3 (PB)
First Published, 1911

2nd Impression 2023

Printed at: Gyan Press, Delhi.

THE DIVINE ARCHER
Author: F. J. GOULD

THE DIVINE ARCHER

Rama— lifted the bow

THE DIVINE ARCHER

FOUNDED ON THE INDIAN EPIC OF THE RAMAYANA WITH TWO STORIES FROM THE MAHABHARATA

BY

F. J. GOULD

LONDON: J. M. DENT & SONS LTD. 1911

CONTENTS

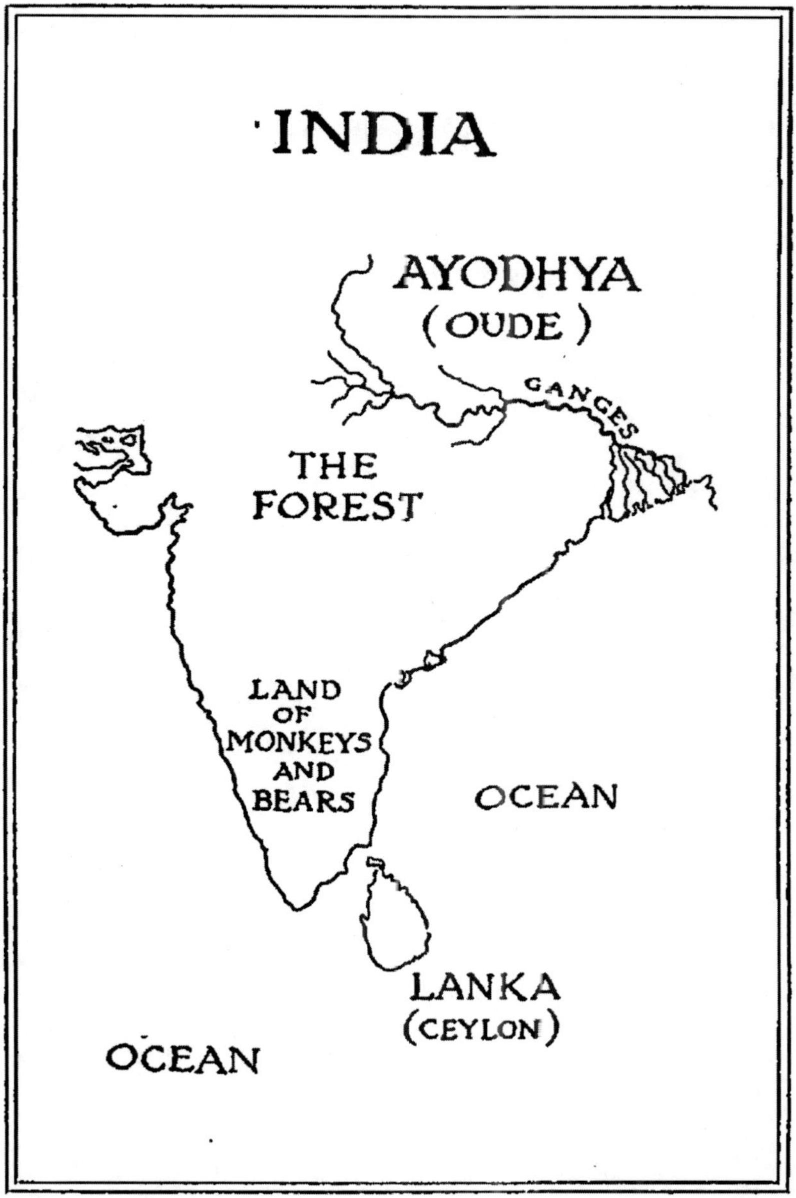

MAP ILLUSTRATING THESE STORIES

PREFATORY NOTE

SPEAKING of the memories of Rama and Sita, so cherished by the Hindu people, Miss Margaret Noble (*Web of Indian Life*) says:—

We ask in vain what can have been the life of India before she found refuge and direction in such dreams as these. For to-day it has become so one with them that all trace of the dawn before they were is lost. They penetrate to every part of the country, every class of society, every grade of education. Journeying in the mountains at nightfall, one came upon the small, open hut of the grain-dealer, and saw, round a tiny lamp, a boy reading the *Ramayana* in the vernacular to a circle of his elders. At the end of each stanza they bowed their heads to the earth, with the chant, "To dear Sita's bridegroom, great Rama, all hail!" The shopkeeper in the city counts out his wares to the customer, saying:

"One (Ram), two (Ram), three (Ram)," and so on, relapsing into a dream of worship when the measuring is done. Nay, once at least it is told how at the "Four (Ram)," the blessed name was enough to touch the inmost soul of him who uttered it, and he rose up then and there and left the world behind him.

The women, terrified at thunder, call on "Sita Ram!" and the bearers of the dead keep time to the cry of "Nama Rama Sattva hai." ("The name of the Lord alone is real.")

THE DIVINE ARCHER

I

FLOWERS were falling from the sky, for the shining gods were happy. And happy also were the folk of the city of Oude, or Ayodhya. Banners waved. Wreaths were hung at every point. Women carried gold and silver dishes laden with gifts to the new-born son of the king. Players of musical instruments marched through the streets. None could tread without stepping on sweet musk and sandalwood and saffron that had been flung upon the ground.

King Dasa-ratha, in his joy, gave presents to the holy priests, the Brahmans—presents of gold and plate, and sacred cows.

The people everywhere brought out rich jewels to adorn the walls of the houses, and the city was all ablaze with gold, silver, red rubies, green emeralds, blue sapphires, and gleaming pearls.

For four weeks the sun forgot to set, and he beamed on the city where the four babes—four sons of the king—were born.

One was son of Queen Kausalya, namely, Rama the Delight; and he was dark.

One was son of Queen Kaikeyi, namely, Bharat; and he was also dark.

The third and fourth were sons of Queen Samitra, namely, Lakshman and Satrughna; and both were fair.

Now, Rama (Rah-ma) was the noblest. On the soles of his feet were the magic signs —the thunderbolt, the flag, and the goad which drivers use to urge elephants. Anklets tinkled on his ankles. A row of tiger's claws were hung across his breast, and a necklace of gems with a charm fastened to it enriched his neck. Curls adorned his head. Clad in wee yellow drawers, the little Indian prince crawled and played; and his mother caught him up, and kissed him, and put him in the cradle, and took him out, and called him the darling of darlings.

But one day, as she and the babe were alone, she saw him change, and he grew, and he grew, and he grew, until he seemed to fill the whole world; ay, and more than that; for not only were hills and woods and streams and seas all about his body, but even suns and moons and stars shone; and yet, in this wide sky and earth, she could still see her baby Rama. Thus for a while he was so great that he could not be greater; and then he changed to the small child again.

Such eyes have mothers; they see into the years to come, and say to themselves, "My child will be noble."

Rama could play and jest, and, while the king and the queen sat at table, he would snatch up a handful of cream and curds and run away, thrusting the dainty into his mouth, and laughing. And all the royal court laughed.

Rama could work. When he and his brethren were grown lads they became twice-born, and sacred threads were placed on each — the thread passing over one shoulder and lying on the breast. Then they went to the Guru, or teacher, to be taught in the book of hymns to the shining gods; and Rama learned the *Vedas* in a very short time — even all the four books of hymns. The four brothers also took lessons in shooting arrows from the bow, and other lessons in something far better, namely, the right behaviour towards men, women, and children. The manners of Prince

Rama were so gentle and so courteous that all the city loved him, and the eyes of the folk followed him as he went along the highway.

Now, in the forest, near the city, there lived an aged hermit, Visva-mitra; and this good old man was sore beset by ugly Furies or Demons, who would not let him rest.

"I will go to the king," he said to himself, "and ask him for the help of his brave son, Rama."

When the hermit stood at the royal gate, the king made haste, and he set the old man on the throne, and brought water to wash his feet, and bowing before him, he said:

"It is a blessed day for me because you have come to my house. Tell me, O holy one, why you come to see me."

"King," he answered, "a troop of furies annoy me in my house in the jungle, and I beg for the aid of your noble son Rama, in driving them away, and let Lakshman the Fortunate come with him."

Then was the face of the king downcast, and he sighed:

"Oh, sir, ask anything but that—cattle, jewels, even myself, but I cannot let my sweet son go. What would his strength avail against the demons of the wood?"

But the wise man of the court, even Vasishta, bade the king send his sons, and so Dasaratha gave way; and having said good-bye to their mothers, they went forth. Each youth was bright of eye, broad of chest; and each had a quiver slung from a yellow sash, and each bore a bow.

A scream was heard on the road, and the hermit pointed to a horrid figure that fluttered in the air.

The Divine Archer, Rama, aimed and shot; and the demon fell, pierced by an arrow.

That night the two princes supped on roots and fruit and water in the hermit's hut, and there also they slept.

At daybreak the hermits of the forest were standing about the fire of sacrifice, when dark shapes floated about their heads, and raised a dreadful yell.

The Divine Archer and his brother raised their bows. Arrows flew; and ere long all the band of demons were slain.

After a few days the hermit, Visva-mitra, said to the young men:

"My lords, would it not gladden your hearts to see the holy stream of Ganges, and to see the city of Videha, where lies the bow that no man on earth can bend?"

"We do, indeed, desire to behold these things," they replied.

So the old man and the two youths fared forth.

They saluted the waters of the Ganges, and bathed in the sacred river.

They journeyed onward and saw the mighty walls and towers of the city of Videha, and round the city were beautiful gardens; and in the city the bazaars were filled with rich goods; and horses, elephants, and chariots crowded the streets; and fountains glittered in the sunshine.

The king of that place was Janak, and he heard of the coming of the hermit, and went to see him as he sat in a grove of mango-trees near the gate, and he kneeled before him in deep respect, and offered him and his companions a fair lodging in the town. So they took up their abode in the rooms which the king placed at their service, and they ate supper.

The sun had not yet set, and Rama saw that his brother Lakshman had a keen longing to view the wonders of the city, so he asked leave of Visva-mitra, and, with the hermit's consent, they walked out into the streets.

As they crossed the market-place, crowds of people, young and old, watched them with wondering looks; for the princes were handsome; they were clothed in yellow coats; their breasts were shining with big pearls; curly hair peeped out from under their caps; they carried bows and arrows in their hands. And Indian girls, peeping from latticed windows, whispered to one another that these princes were goodly youths, and surely the dark one was fit for wedding with the king's daughter, Sita (Seeta).

Thus they rambled from street to street till they arrived at the meadow of sports—a vast place marked out in a ring; and all round it were, first, a row of seats for princes and nobles; then behind that, higher up, a row of seats for the citizens; and a grand gallery, painted in many colours, was the Place of Ladies. All was quiet, and after giving a hasty look at this tournament field, the brothers hurried to their lodging, and were soon asleep.

At the rising of the sun Rama and Lakshman bathed in a stream, and asked the hermit if they might pluck flowers, and he cheerfully gave leave.

Now, as they roved, they saw the splendid garden of the king, and they entered and admired the fruit trees and the flowers, and the peacocks, which spread their glorious tails; and they came to a lake like a looking-glass, around which were steps of smooth stone; and water-hens plashed in the pool, and thousands of lilies—which the Hindus name the lotus—spread their lovely petals to the sun. And the gardeners allowed the princes to cut flowers. And it came to pass that the Princess Sita was walking in the garden with her maids. One of the maids had gone in front of the others, and she suddenly saw the two youths. She paused one moment, and then ran back.

"What have you seen?" asked her companions.

"I have seen two most noble youths."

II

At that instant, Rama heard the jingle of the bangles on the lady Sita's feet, and he said:

"I know of a surety that there comes hither a lady whom I shall love beyond all things else in the world."

Lifting his eyes he saw Sita, the king's daughter, and they loved each other then and for ever.

The princess said not a word.

"It is time to go," said one of the maids. "Let us return to the palace, Lady Sita."

"It is time to go," echoed the princess; and presently she and her companions had passed from view of the brothers.

On the way to the palace, she stopped at the house of the goddess Bhavani, and, entering the temple, she knelt before the image and prayed—

"Great mother, bright as the lightning; and giver of gifts to gods and men, thou knowest, as I bend before thy lotus feet, what is the wish of my heart."

Then a garland of flowers dropped from the

hand of the image, and Sita picked it up with joy, and felt a throb in her left side, and was sure, by these tokens, that her prayer was heard.

With flowers in hand, the princes returned to the guru, and told him of the meeting in the king's garden. The sage recited holy legends during the day, and at night Rama lifted his eyes to the moon and said:

"The queen of night is not so fair as Sita."

Next day vast crowds flocked to the green space where the trial of the bow was to be held. Murmurs arose from the people when the two princes of Ayodhya took their seats. Kings were there who had come to bend the bow of the god Siva, and they looked with jealous eyes at the brothers; but Sita gazed at Rama with a look of delight. Folk whispered:

"The dark youth is the right husband for Sita."

Heralds cried aloud:

"Here is the great bow of the god, and he who shall bend it will have fame in earth and heaven and hell, and take the king's daughter to wife."

One king after another mounted the platform and girded up his loins, and pulled, tugged, strained. . . .

All in vain.

" Well," said King Janak, with a sneer, " if I had known there were no men in the world, I would not have come to this spot to be laughed at for offering what no one will take."

" No men in the world! " said Lakshman to his brother, " we must not let this wretched old bow mock us."

The hermit spoke a word in Rama's ear:

" Up, Rama, and break the bow! "

Rama bowed at the feet of the sage, and went up on the platform.

Lakshman muttered a prayer:

" O ye elephants that hold up the four quarters of the world, and O tortoise, upon whom the elephants stand, hold the earth firm when the bow breaks, for mighty will be the shock."

The people stood still and silent. A tear trembled in the eye of Sita.

Flashing with light, the bow gleamed in Rama's hand. When he bent it, lo! it seemed to bend over all the sky.

It snapped with a crash.

The crash shook the earth, the elephants, the tortoise, and even the shining gods put their hands to their ears, so loud was the rumbling!

People shouted. Angels danced in the sky. The gods rained down gay flowers, and the kettle-drums rolled in heaven; and on earth the citizens made noises with cymbals, drums, conch-shells, clarions, and sackbuts; and women sang songs.

Some of the kings growled like surly tigers, and grasped their weapons, as if they would do harm to Rama.

But just then a strange and weird figure sprang upon the scene. It was a tall, bull-like man who had a bow in one hand, and had tilted an axe over his shoulder. His body was bare except for a deerskin cloth about his loins. On his brow were marked three white lines that showed he worshipped the god Siva. His hair was twisted in a knot. Flushed with rage, this hermit of the woods had come to see who had broken the god's bow.

The whole crowd bowed to him, for his name was a name of terror to all the land.

"Who has broken the bow?" he thundered.

"'Twas an old bow," replied Lakshman, "which my brother snapped. Why be angry?"

"Wretch!" shrieked the hermit, "do you talk thus of the sacred bow? Know you not that with my axe I cut off the thousand arms of a fiend?"

"Holy sir," said Lakshman, "do not blow at me as if I could be puffed away."

"The madman who dares thus to speak shall be swallowed by the jaws of death!"

The hermit would have smitten the youth with his terrible axe, but Rama stepped between, put his hands together in sign of respect, and sought by soft words to turn away the sage's wrath.

"If," said the hermit at last, "you are a hero indeed, draw this bow of Vishnu."

So saying, he handed to Rama his bow, the string hanging loose. No sooner had Rama touched it than the string fastened itself tight, ready for shooting a shaft!

At this token of magic the hermit of the woods clasped his hands in homage:

"Glory to the mighty Rama!"

And he went his way, and the kings also departed. Then was the city made glorious with ornaments—arches set up in the streets, and pillars of gold crusted with green emeralds, and wreaths of lilies made out of pearls, turquoises, and diamonds, and golden birds and golden bees that were hung amid the leaves of trees. For Rama was to marry Sita, and nothing could be too splendid to express the people's gladness.

Messengers sped to the city of Ayodhya to tell the old King Dasa-ratha of the breaking of the bow and of the coming marriage, and to bid him travel in all haste to the bridal.

Amid the joyful cheers of the citizens, King Dasa-ratha set forth in procession—soldiers on grand horses, nobles on the backs of elephants, and over the heads of the nobles were spread canopies; and the elephants' bells jangled, and the drums beat; and three million porters carried the baggage of the royal party; and the sky rained flowers, and the gods beat their kettle-drums.

A blue-necked jay pecked seed on the road. It was a token of good fortune!

A woman passed with a child and a pitcher. Another good omen!

A man carried fish and curds of milk! Another happy token.

Two Brahmans met the procession, and each held a book. Another pleasing presage!

As the procession arrived at the gates of the city of Videha, out came an army of servants with gifts—clothes, jewels, birds, deer, horses, elephants, chariots, spices, perfumes; and cakes on silver trays and dainties on golden dishes. And they all marched in together; and the sky rained flowers, and the kettle-drums of the gods rattled.

Blissful was the meeting of King Dasa-ratha with his two noble sons and the good hermit of the jungle, Visva-mitra.

On the bridal-day, Rama, clad in dazzling raiment, rode on horseback, and the saddle glittered with pearls and rubies, and the harness glowed like the sun; and so, amid the music of bells and trumpets and voices, Rama entered the great pavilion. And when all the nobles were in their places the bride came in with her maids, and the sweet bells on their ankles tinkled. Prayers were said, the flame of the altar burned heavenwards; the bride and bridegroom walked, hand-in-hand, round the altar three times.

Nay, I should have said the brides and bridegrooms, for on that same day, in that same place, the three brothers of Rama were married to three lovely ladies, and thus the wedding was four-fold.

Walking over the beautiful carpets, the guests proceeded to the banquet, and all were merry at the tables, and music clashed, and laughter rose to the roof.

Many days the gaiety lasted, and when the King of Ayodhya and his four sons and their four brides must needs go home, vast were the gifts given them by King Janak—100,000 horses, 25,000 chariots, 10,000 elephants; waggons of gold and jewels; buffaloes and cows without number.

The sky rained flowers.

The sacred kettle-drums rolled.

III

ONE day, King Dasa-ratha, looking in a polished mirror in order to set his crown straight, saw a white hair.

The white hair whispered:

"O King, old age comes on. Make Rama regent, and you will be happy in seeing the noble way in which he acts the part of monarch."

First he spoke his thought to the guru—the teacher; and the guru said:

"Yes, O King, let this thing be done without delay; yes, this very morrow."

Tidings were sent round the city of Ayodhya that on the next day the Prince Rama would be made king, and the people, who all loved Rama, every man, every woman, every child, prepared banners and canopies, and imitation fruit-trees sparkling with jewels to adorn the streets; and all night the busy hands were at the work.

Now, at this time two of the four princes—Bharat and Satrughna—were in the region of the West.

You may remember that Bharat had not the same mother as Rama. His mother was Queen Kaikeyi.

On the night when the citizens were putting up the shining jewel-trees in the streets, and the strains of music were heard in every quarter of Ayodhya, a dark and ugly face peered forth from a window in that part of the palace where lived Queen Kaikeyi. The face was that of the hump-backed waiting-woman, Manthara. Leaning out of the lattice, she said to some folk that passed:

"What mean the songs and the sparkling lights?"

"Have you not heard? The glorious Rama, breaker of the bow of the god, is to be made king in his father's stead to-morrow."

Manthara drew in her head quickly, and she stood still and thought a long time.

Oh! the evil thoughts that swarmed in Manthara's brain! Alas, for the sorrow that was to come upon Rama, and Sita, and Lakshman, and Bharat, and the old king, and the city, and upon hosts and hosts of the folk of India! Woe to Rama! Years must pass before joy shines again upon the city, and before the festal music is heard in the streets and the jewel-trees grow in the highways.

The waiting-woman lifted the curtain of Queen Kaikeyi's door, and tottered in crying and wringing her hands.

"What is the matter?" asked the queen.

She still cried.

"Is Rama ill, or my Bharat?"

"Do not speak tenderly of Rama! Why should he be made king to-morrow? For so all the city says he will. And look from the lattice, queen, and see the people preparing for the festival. Why did the king send your beloved son, Bharat, away? Was it not at the wish of the vile Queen Kausalya, mother of Rama, in order that her own child should be raised to honour? What will happen to you and your son? You will be caught like a fly in a bowl of milk. You will be bondslaves to this proud Rama."

"Now I understand," said the queen with a frown, "why my right eye keeps throbbing, and I have bad dreams at night. What shall I do, dear and trusted friend?"

"Go, mistress, to the dark chamber, where, as the king knows, his ladies retire when they are smit with sorrow. Let Dasa-ratha find you lying on the floor."

Joyous citizens came and went in and out of the palace. On all sides shouts of mirth resounded. The king was as happy as the love-god. With light foot he approached Queen Kaikeyi's room.

" She is in the sulking chamber, sir," said the hump-backed waiting-woman.

With a mind sore disturbed, Dasa-ratha hastened to the dark room. By a dim lamp, he saw his queen lying on the floor, her dress being old and coarse, and her hair all wild.

" Why are you angry, joy of my soul? " he asked.

She glared at him like a snake, and put out her arms to bid him keep away.

" Rise, my dear, this is no time for ill-temper, for on the morrow I give the throne to my noble son Rama. Come and rejoice with us."

" I cannot. Once you promised me two boons, and you have never given me them. To Rama you give all; to me, naught."

" Nay, queen, I will keep my word like a king. Deck yourself in comely robes, and I will grant you the two favours, whatsoever they are."

She changed her dress, and put on her glinting gems, and said with a smile:

"Dasa-ratha, make our son Bharat king; that is one boon. Send Rama into a far land for fourteen years; that is the other boon. You have pledged your word as a king."

He put his hands to his forehead and trembled, even as a partridge that is pounced upon by a falcon in the forest.

"Now," he moaned, "now has my wife laid waste the city of Oude, and brought woe upon my paradise. How can I live without Rama?"

"If," she shrieked, "if at daybreak to-morrow, Rama does not leave the city, clad in the hermit's coarse robe, know, O Dasa-ratha, it will be the death of me, and everlasting disgrace will come upon your head."

And though he knelt and prayed at her feet, she would not change her will.

So passed his night in grief, and the music still rang in the streets, but there was no music in the king's heart.

Rama rose very early and saw his father lying as in a swoon on the ground.

"What ails him?" he asked of queen Kaikeyi.

With cruel looks in her eyes, she told him, and waited to see him act like a raging madman.

But Rama said in a clear, steady voice:

"It is well, O queen. Often have I longed to dwell in the peaceful forest, and thither will I go."

"Father," he said, as the king revived at the sound of his son's voice, "I go to bid my mother farewell."

When Rama appeared before Kausalya, she beamed with joy.

"My darling," she cried, "this is the happy day."

Gently, he broke in:—

"Mother, my father has given me a kingdom."

"Yes, my son, the kingdom of Ayodhya."

"No, mother, the kingdom of the wild woods, where I am to dwell for fourteen years, while Bharat reigns as king."

Then was the queen's soul torn sharp with

grief, and she clung to his feet—his lotus-feet—and wept much; and as she wept, there came in the lady Sita, to hear the mournful news. And Sita, for a time, shed tears, and was silent.

"But do not take Sita," begged the mother.

"Dear Sita," said Rama, "for my mother's sake, you will stay here."

"No," she answered, "as a river without water, so is a wife without her husband. The birds and the deer shall be my comrades, the forest my dwelling, the bark of the trees my dress. The hut we live in together will be even as a mansion of the gods, and the road that we two walk will not make me weary."

And as Sita said, so also said Lakshman, for he declared that he would share the long banishment with his brother, just as he had shared his joys.

These three then went to say good-bye to the king; and the king's heart was like to break. And as they talked together, the Queen Kaikeyi entered with a box, and, setting it on the ground, she opened it, and there lay in it the coarse dark coat of a hermit.

"I have brought you your raiment," she said, with a dreadful smile.

Rama put it on and bowed to his father and to Kaikeyi, and left the palace, and the people saw him go forth.

The jewel-trees were hid away; the banners all torn down; hushed were all songs; for the tidings had gone about the city that Rama was to live in an exile of fourteen years.

"Sir," said Rama to his guru, "be kind to all my servants while I am away."

So saying, he went out with Sita and Lakshman, and many people of the city ran at their side and in front and behind—old and young, and children; and the sobs of the folk were sad to hear.

IV

NOT only did the folk mourn. The very trees withered, and the horses, elephants, and birds seemed to feel the loss of a prince who had been the friend of every citizen and every dumb creature in Ayodhya. Rama, Lakshman, Sita, and the people travelled all the day, and at night all except the three exiles slept soundly under the trees.

The three exiles mounted their chariot in the darkness, lest the people should follow again, and be worn out.

On coming to the holy Ganges in the morning, they saluted the noble flood which all India worships, and bathed in its refreshing waters.

A crowd of people approached with gifts of fruit, for they had heard of the journey of the princes.

"Pray," invited the leader, "lodge in my house to-night."

"For fourteen years," replied Rama, "must we abide in the open air, nor enter any village."

The good man then spread a mat of grass and soft leaves under a sinsapa tree, and this was the couch of the wanderers that second night. At break of day, Rama sent away the chariot, though the charioteer begged them to ride to the city, for he was sure the old king wished it.

The horses loved Rama, and whinneyed and turned their heads towards him as they departed.

Now they must cross the Ganges. An old

ferryman took them over the rolling stream, and would not take for fee the ring which Sita drew from her finger.

"No," he said, "pay me when you come back—in fourteen years from now."

Sita spoke to the sacred Ganges.

"O river, may I return with my husband and his brother and again adore you."

"Lady," said the great river, "you will all return in safety and again cross my waves."

They came to the mighty forest. Here and there they passed a hermit's hut, sheltered under tall trees. Rama walked first, then Sita, then Lakshman. Birds and deer looked upon them as they threaded their way through the jungle. At night they rested under a fig-tree.

Next day they reached the hut of the hermit Valmiki. It was built near a spring of clear water, which formed a pool, and lotuses made the water pretty. The forest trees were bright with blossoms, and bees hummed in a sweet murmur.

Old Valmiki sat with them in his hut, and heard the story of their exile from Ayodhya. Then he pointed to a hill.

"On yonder hill of Chitra-Kuta," he said, "you should make your abode. A river winds about its slope. There, amid the woods, dwell in a green shelter, and elephants, tigers, lions, monkeys, boars, deer, and birds will be your friends and companions."

So in the green cot on Chitra-Kuta they lodged; and the flowers bloomed gaily, and the wild beasts were pleasant comrades, and jays, cuckoos, parrots, and many other feathered friends made good company.

Meanwhile, the charioteer had gone back to the city, and told the King Dasa-ratha all that had happened.

Death of the King

The king lay on a sick-bed, his wife, Kausalya, at his side. When he had heard the charioteer's report, he sent him away and said to his wife:

"Now, dear wife, I call to mind the curse of the blind hermit, for he told me I should weep for a beloved son, even as I caused him to weep."

"How did you give him cause to weep?" asked the queen.

"In this way did it come to pass," said the king. "When I was a young hunter, so keen was my sense of hearing that I could aim at a beast in the dark and kill it, simply by hearing the sound of its tread, and judging in what spot it was to be found. People called me the Shooter in the Dark, and proud was I of the title. One night, before I ever met you, dear Kausalya, I rode out in my chariot to the woods where beasts were wont to drink at the woodland pool, and I lay in wait. At last I heard a rustle and a splash. I felt sure it was an elephant on the bank of the lake. So I fitted an arrow to my bow, and shot. Alas! The cry of some one hurt—a human cry—smote on my ear. What had I done? I made haste through the shrubs and trees, and by the dim star-light I saw on the bank of the water a youth who was bleeding, and a pitcher lay at his side. He asked me what ill deed he had done that I should take his life. His parents were old folk, both blind. They lived in yonder humble shed. He felt he was dying, but, with his last breath, bade me go and tell his mother and father what had happened. So I left him dead, and, with a heavy heart, made my way to the hut. The old folks heard my steps. The father called out to ask why I had been so long, for he thought his son had returned. So I told them the tale of sorrow and death, and prayed for their pardon, because I had slain their son unknowingly. They bade me lead them to the place of the dead, and, with trembling hands poured funeral water over the body, crooned a holy song of farewell, and dropped many a tear. Then the old hermit said that, for a punishment, I, too, should suffer as he had suffered. I should bewail the loss of a dearly loved son."

At midnight the king blessed his wife, Kausalya, and blessed his wife, Samitra, mother of Lakshman (but he did not bless Kaikeyi), and he died.

. . . . . .

In the Western land, word came to Prince Bharat that the guru bade him repair to the city. At once he leaped into a chariot.

"O that I had wings to fly," he cried.

Horses tore; wheels rattled.

Queen Kaikeyi met her son.

"Is my father well?"

" He is dead, my son."

" Alas! my father, my father. How came he to die so soon? "

She told him all about the exiles; that he—Bharat—was now king; thanks to the faithful humpback, Manthara.

" Wretched woman! " he shouted. " Why did the king—good sire that he was—give way to you? And you, base creature, what led you to this vile plot? I loved Rama as I loved myself."

So crying, and half-mad with grief, he pushed Manthara till she reeled, and then he fled from the room to the chamber of Kausalya. His brother, Satrughna, went with him; and all wept together.

A vast pile of sandal-wood and aloes and spices was heaped up beside the river, and the royal body was laid thereon, and the fire leaped to heaven.

After the funeral, Bharat, the noble prince, announced his will. He would go to the woods, and bring Rama back, and all who pleased might go with him on his errand. Deep was the joy in every house, and folk went forth on horses and elephants, in carts and chariots

—high and low, rich and poor—in one great eager stream. Point by point they tracked the pilgrims—to the sinsapa tree; to the Ganges; to the jungle; to the hut of old white-haired Valmiki, until at last, the procession of citizens halted at the holy hill of Chitra-Kuta, and looked with wondering eyes upon the scene.

Rocks rose high, and splendid trees clothed them with their shade. Wild animals lay or moved about or ate together in peace—hares, elephants, lions, tigers, boars, buffaloes, wolves; and bees hummed; and parrots chattered, and peacocks spread their glorious tails. And in the midst stood Rama, Sita, and Lakshman.

Happy were the moments of meeting, but grief followed. For neither to the pleading of Bharat, nor the tears of his mother, Kausalya, would the noble Rama yield. His father, he said, had commanded him into exile, and in exile he would stay; and Bharat must rule the kingdom.

And so, after many words said on each side, Bharat and the citizens and the Queen Kausalya returned to Ayodhya. But Bharat took with him as a keepsake a pair of sandals which Rama had worn; and he put these shoes on the golden throne in the palace, to wait there until his brother came home.

V

ONE day the glorious Rama, thinking the people of Ayodhya would never let him rest in the green shades of the hill of Chitra-Kuta, set forth again on his wanderings with the lady Sita and the loyal Lakshman, and plunged into the depths of the forest. Tall were the trees; glowing the hues of the flowers; fair the lotuses on the pools; and when there was a space among the boughs, and the sun's rays fell through, beautiful were the spots of light in the glades of the wood. And save for the call of the birds, or the rustle of beasts amid the foliage, or the ripple of brooks, very quiet was the forest. Now and then the pilgrims halted at the hut of some saintly hermit, and talked with him of love and mercy and justice and the service of the gods.

Such a hermit was Saint Agastya, a brave man who had come from the north of India to seek out the wild tribes of the Deccan, that so he might speak to them words of grace and truth, and teach them to be more humane and gentle in their dealings. As he greeted the wanderers, he had comrades at his right hand and his left—holy hermits who helped him in his work, and fed the flames on altars in honour of the god Brahm, and fiery Agni, and shining Vishnu, and Yama, Lord of Death, and Dharma, the god of well-doing. And Saint Agastya looked upon Rama and loved him, and he gave him rare gifts. He gave him the magic bow of the lord Vishnu, and the glittering dart of Brahma, and the quiver of Indra that never lacked arrows, no matter how often shafts were shot, and, last of all, a sabre with a hilt of gold. Well armed was now the Divine Archer.

" Rama," he said in words deep in meaning, " you will have need of these weapons."

" I thank you with all my heart, great sage, and much would I like to stay in this charming spot. But the fate of exile rests upon us, and we must go still further."

"I will tell you a place where you may be quite alone, except for the roving deer. Walk through that thick wood until you see an old nyagrodha tree, then climb a steep path, and so you will come to a stand in the forest of Panchavati, where the Godaveri stream rushes along the dark glen."

Near the glen, Lakshman built a house for the winter that was coming. The walls were of soft earth, the posts of bamboo, thatch of jungle leaves and grass; and the floor was stamped upon and pressed till it was quite level. And here they dwelt in peace while autumn glided by, and when the winter night air was cold; berries their food and water their drink. Oft they talked of home and the people of Ayodhya, and of times that seemed far back in mists, when Rama broke the bow of Siva, and the thunders of the cheers shook the city of Videha. In the woods how still was the scene, how lonely the paths; and yet the three hearts were good and tender comrades to each other, and they worshipped the red sun at dawn and at eve, and so the winter went by in peace.

One day a wild-looking woman met the lord

Rama in the wood of Panchavati; her face tanned by air and sun; her hair loose; her mouth ape-like and cruel.

She was a Raksha—a demon maid; and she admired the noble form of Rama.

"Who are you that wander in the forest that belongs to us Rakshas, to me, and to my brothers Khara and Dushan?"

Rama told her the tale of the exile.

"Wander no more," she said; "make your home with us demons of the jungle. You shall be my husband, and our food shall be the flesh of men."

"My dear wife is Sita," he answered, "and not for me is the horrid food that pleases Rakshas. But my brother has no wife."

This he said with a smile.

To Lakshman then she went, and said like words, and when he said No in a very angry voice, she took on a terrible shape, and her eyes glared, and Lakshman, in swift swing of his sword, slashed the Raksha's nose and ears, and she fled shrieking to her brothers.

Presently Rama shouted to Lakshman:

"Take Sita to the nearest cave and shield her there. The Raksha army is flying this way."

Black figures were gathering in the air, thousands upon thousands; and the yell of the Rakshas was like the noise of a storm at sea. But when the two demon captains first beheld the shining body and steady eyes of Rama, they paused in dread, for in the moment of battle, Rama shone even as the sun.

They sent messengers who said:

"Prince, give up your wife as prisoner, and you and your brother may go free."

Rama gave back words of scorn; and then, with a howl, and waving clubs, spikes, spears, scimitars, maces, axes, and bows, the Rakshas advanced. As arrows fell towards Rama he swung his sabre — the gold-hilted sabre — in such wise as to cut them all in twain though they rained in countless swarms. Then he bent the bow of Vishnu, and took arrows from the quiver that never was empty, and he shot and shot and shot and shot, and the air was filled with arrows, and the Rakshas fell and sprang up again, and rushed upon him and fled, and vultures flew down to eat the slain, and lo! the battle came to a sudden end. Rama stood over the dead army, and he was calm in hand and eye; and the gods dropped flowers from the sky, and sweet music rang in the air.

And the souls of the Rakshas went up to the house of the gods; for such was the way in the old Indian days, and when a foe was beaten by a noble prince, his death was thought to be enough, and the great-hearted conquerors let the souls of the conquered go to the place of peace; even the souls of the bad.

Sita came out of the cave and embraced her prince.

But the Raksha woman sped from the forest of Panchavati, and it was woe to poor Sita that she went that journey. For the Raksha woman crossed the water on the south shore of India, and hastened to the palace of her great brother, Ravan, King of the Rakshas of Lanka. Now Lanka was the island of Ceylon. And Ravan was the most gruesome monster on earth, for he had ten heads and twenty hands.

"Who can this archer be?" Ravan muttered to himself. "I must measure my strength with his, and see who is the better warrior, and deeper in wit."

He sought out his cunning friend Maricha.

"Comrade, I want your help. You must take the shape of a beautiful deer, and show yourself to my enemy, and lure him away from his lady, Sita; and I will seize her and bring her to this island of the Rakshas."

Little did Maricha care for the task, for he knew the power of Rama; but he also knew the power of Ravan the Ten-headed, and so he consented, and the two demons made their way in easy flight to the far-off forest by the silver stream of Godaveri.

Sita suddenly called to Rama:

"See, my prince! What a lovely creature comes towards us."

It was a deer with a skin like burnished gold, and on its branching antlers it bore blue sapphires.

"I beg you," cried Sita, "to get me this animal's skin, and some day, when we go home, it shall adorn our palace in Ayodhya."

So Rama, willing to please his wife, gave chase to the deer, while Lakshman stayed at her side. The deer (which was the cunning Maricha) flew this way and that, and slipped into dark nooks, and away into crooked glades, and into dells, and up cliffs, and Rama had much work to come at it, and far off was he when it fell by his deadly shaft.

"Hark!" said Sita. "What was that?"

It was a sound as of Rama's voice.

"I am hurt, Lakshman. Come to my aid!"

"Quick!" she cried to Lakshman.

VI

LAKSHMAN stood still.

"I ought not," he said, "to leave you alone in this jungle. Do not fear for Rama. He has no equal in the world for strength and wit."

"Crafty man," burst out Sita, "do you wish Rama to die in order that you may have his wife?"

Cruel was the word. In all her life Sita scarce said a word that hurt a human soul, or made the heart of a dumb animal quail. But this word was indeed harsh.

And ah! bitter, bitter, thrice bitter was the fate that fell on Sita for her fault.

Lakshman turned and went; and many a long day passed ere he saw her face again.

An old hermit of the forest stood amid the trees, and he bowed to Sita.

An old hermit, did I say? It was the Demon King of Lanka, Ravan, the Ten-headed and Twenty-handed, in a guise that the lady knew not.

"Fair stranger," he said humbly, "are you a nymph of the woodland? Whatever you are—you with your ruddy lips, your pearly teeth, your dark, shiny tresses—you are more meet for a royal mansion than this weird haunt of wild beasts, and of horrid Rakshas."

"I am Sita, the daughter of King Janak," she answered, "and through the working of an evil woman, my husband, Rama, and I have been sent into exile. And who, sir, are you?"

"No guru am I," he replied, with a wicked laugh. "I am the lord of the Rakshas of Ceylon, and much do I want a queen like you. Splendid is my island, and five thousand damsels will wait upon you, Sita, if you will share my throne."

Sparkled the eyes of Sita.

"I—I—I share a demon's throne? I, the wedded wife of the hero Rama—Rama, like to the glorious moon—Rama, the matchless warrior! Tear up yonder mountain, Raksha; you will do that sooner than you will win Rama's spouse!"

Sita shrieked. Ravan had seized her, lifted her into his chariot, and his demon horses fled through the air; and now she saw that Ravan had ten heads and twenty hands—twenty hands to hold the reins of the terrible steeds.

A shrill, rough cry was heard, and a big, old, grey vulture flapped his wings and swooped down towards the flying car.

"Fear not, Sita; fear not, my daughter!" called the king of the vultures, Jatayu.

The giant bird clutched Ravan's hair in his talons, and hurled him like a stone out of the chariot, and he fell with a thud to the ground.

Leaping up, the demon struck with his sabre, and slashed off the vulture's wings, and the poor, faithful bird lay helpless while Ravan rode off in triumph.

"Rama! Rama!" cried Sita.

"Rama! Rama!" cried the croaking voice of the vulture.

. . . . . .

"Where have you left Sita?" asked Rama,

as he stood by the dead golden deer, and saw Lakshman at his side.

"She would insist that I should come, brother."

Rama sprang up like lightning, and ran, ran, ran to the hut.

Sita was gone.

"O ye deer! O bees that hum!" he called aloud in the jungle. "O gliding serpent and roaring lion! O trees and flowers, tell me, where is Sitá?"

The brothers rushed from point to point, till they saw a wingless vulture, and they knelt beside him, for they knew him again as old Jatayu.

"Master," moaned the grey bird, "now I am ready to die, for I have seen your lotus face. Alas! Ravan has carried off your lady, and he has slain your servant—even me."

"Noble bird," said Rama, with faltering voice, "you die; but in dying you fly higher than ever you soared over the Vindhya hills, for you shall go up to the land of the shining gods."

When the old Jatayu had breathed his last, Rama made a funeral pile of wood, and buried the body as if it had been the body of a just man. Unclean and vile as the creature was to the eye, his heart was loyal, and Rama rendered him honour as to a true knight that did his duty.

Wandering onwards, the Divine Archer and his brother, Lakshman, peered eagerly into every corner of the forest that seemed likely to be a hiding-place for the demon-king and his prisoner. Herds of elephants trotted by and trumpeted, and seemed to say—

"She is not here."

And dappled deer scudded by on light feet, and tossed their antlers and seemed to say—

"She is not here."

At the lake of Pampa they stopped. Lovely were the lotuses on the gleaming water, and swans and water-fowl swam from side to side, and geese and cranes flew in great flights overhead. Hermits lived in this charming spot, but none could tell where Sita was.

Now came the sad brothers to the Nilghiri mountains, and not far now was the point of India that runs southward into the broad ocean.

Two singular persons met the two princes of

Ayodhya in the wilderness of these mountains, and wild was their aspect. They were tall, strong monkeys; yet were they as men, with the voices of men, and the speech of men, and the ways of men—not gentle, indeed, as the ways of the citizens of Ayodhya, but still, they were human in their roughness.

Perhaps (to tell the likely truth) these creatures whom the old Indian poet calls monkeys were the uncouth and rude-looking natives of the south land. Monkeys and bears, he says, were the folk of this southern region; and monkeys and bears we will call them in our tale; and yet, all the time, we will try to think of them as brave and honest human beings, who, in spite of their wild manners, were most faithful friends to glorious Rama and his brother.

The two singular persons, then, were Sugriva, king of the monkeys, and Hanuman, his comrade. Now Sugriva had been driven from his kingdom by his brother Bali.

Hanuman pointed to the handsome brothers. "See," he said, "these can be none others than the exiled sons of King Dasa-ratha. They search for the lady Sita. They are in grief, as you are. Let us make compact with them, and offer them our aid."

At the lotus-feet of Rama bowed Sugriva, the monkey-king; and Hanuman, good soul, bowed also, even more lowly than his friend.

"We know your trouble, lord Rama," said the king. "And we beg you to accept our help. It may be that we shall find your wife, for we, wild creatures as we are, understand the ways and wiles of the demons of Lanka."

So Rama grasped the hands of Sugriva, and Hanuman made an altar of earth, and lit a fire on it for the gods to see, and the four friends walked round it in token of the bond of faithfulness.

"Do you know this scarf?" said the chief of the monkeys, as he held a bright ribbon to Rama.

Rama gave a shout of surprise.

"It is my Sita's scarf," he cried. "How got you this?"

"One day, when I was on these hills with my attendants, we heard a rushing in the air, and saw a chariot fly by, and heard a voice call Rama, and this scarf dropped at my feet."

"Sita, Sita," sobbed Rama, as he kissed the scarf.

Soon he dried his tears.

"Now," said Rama, "we must seek the lost one. But first, my friend, I must do you a service, and restore your kingdom to you. Let us go and do battle with Bali."

So they marched to the city where Bali was in power as tyrant. And when news came to him that Rama approached, he took his weapons. His wife clung to him, and implored him not to pit himself against the might of Rama. He took no heed, and boldly sallied forth from the city gates.

VII

Bali and Sugriva fought first, their eyes glowing like red-hot copper. They strove like mad eagles. With claws like tigers they tore up trees and rocks and flung them at each other. Ill would have it fared with Sugriva, however, had not the Divine Archer, Rama, fitted an arrow to his wondrous bow, and shot the tyrant dead.

Sugriva, the monkey-king, could now again take the throne from which his tyrant brother had ousted him; and he begged Rama the Delight to rest a while in his home.

"No," said Rama, "I may not enter a city for fourteen years. But I shall need your friendship soon. Meanwhile, for a few days I will breathe the air of the hills, and prepare for the perilous days that are coming."

In a cave in the Nilghiri mountains the two princes lodged. Coming forth one day upon the hillside, Rama spoke to Lakshman:

"The rains come and go. Dark clouds roll over the blue, and the clap of thunder signals the storm, and the waters of heaven descend, and the streamlets of the hills are swollen. Grass springs up afresh. Frogs croak. Peacocks strut in glory. Bees murmur. Lotuses bloom. The fire-flies glow at dusk. And all the scene is happy, Lakshman; but how can my heart partake of the general joy when my Sita, even now, pines a captive in the den of a Raksha?"

As soon as the days of rain were past, Rama bade King Sugriva come before him with his bright-eyed, tree-climbing monkey folk. In a great army, rank upon rank, legion upon legion, the sprightly monkeys stood—small, stout, short, tall, brown, black. When Rama had told his desire that they should search the land for the lost lady, they started at once, to the north, the south, the east, the west, to forest, to rock, to sea-shore, to cave, to hill, to plain.

The last to leave was brave Hanuman.

"Take this ring," said Rama to the faithful ape, as he drew a bright circlet of gold from his finger, "and if you find my Sita, give her this in token that I never lose the thought of her, and that I will surely come to save her."

Far and wide had the monkeys gone in their quest, and none had found the wife of Rama. A party of searchers—Hanuman among them—at length stood on the shore of the sea that rippled in purple waves between India and the Island of Ceylon.

A huge vulture flapped its wings, and it spoke to Hanuman:

"The vultures, O Hanuman, are loving friends of Rama, and I will tell you what I, with a vulture's keen vision, can see. As I look across the water from here, I can see

Sita weeping in a grove of asoka trees in Lanka. Whoever can leap over the water will find her in the garden of the demon-king."

Hanuman told his companions he would make the venture. Between India and Lanka the passage is more than thirty miles wide, and in the water lie rocks that make a sort of bridge—Adam's bridge, folk call it to-day. The monkey resolved to leap from rock to rock, or rather fly; for he had more than a common monkey's strength; he had powers of magic.

An enormous serpent rose up against him just as he was about to depart, its mouth yawning like a cave. Hanuman's body swelled larger than the serpent's jaws. The reptile's mouth doubled its size. Hanuman's size also doubled! Presently, the monkey mocked his foe by making himself small and darting right into the serpent's mouth, and out again!

"Hanuman," said the serpent, "the gods only sent me to try your courage. You have stood the test. Proceed on your errand of mercy."

In vast jumps, Hanuman leaped from rock

to rock, the air whistling round his head, the waters of the ocean rolling below.

The monkey alighted on a tall peak, whence he saw the splendid city of the demon chief. The walls were of glistening gold, inside which were streets, bazaars, elephants, horses, mules, chariots, gardens, groves, lawns, and ponds. Demons crowded the ways and spaces—demons with the heads of men, buffaloes, oxen, asses, and goats.

Hanuman made himself as tiny as a gnat, flew into the city, unseen by the guards, and roved from one scene to another, admiring the riches and the greatness of it all. At length his eye caught the name of RAMA on the wall of a fine building. He entered (now being in his proper shape), and met a grave, noble-looking man, very different from the demons of Lanka.

"I rejoice," said the monkey chief, "to find some one here who loves the name of Rama. Who, sir, may you be?"

"I am Vibishan, brother to the ten-headed king. But I have no care for the things he cares for, and my heart is not in Lanka at all, and often I wish I were afar off in Ayodhya, where I should be comrade to the noble Rama. And who are you?"

Hanuman told all the tale of Rama and Sita and the search.

"Friend," said Vibishan, pointing, "in yonder grove of asoka trees is a mansion. There Sita is kept a prisoner."

The faithful monkey rushed off at once, and halted under the shade of the asoka trees, just as the lady Sita came out into the garden, pale and sad; and her dark hair was twisted in one braid and knotted, as a sign of mourning for her absent lord.

A noise was heard. Ravan, the ten-headed and twenty-handed king, entered the grounds, with a troop of demon waiting-women.

"Once again, lady," he said harshly, "I ask you if you will become my queen."

"Never."

"You shall be queen above all my other queens."

"Never. My lord Rama will come and save me."

"He will not, for you shall die."

He raised his blue-steel scimitar.

"Yes, Ravan, kill me, and rid me of my sorrow."

But there was a power in her eyes that held his hand. He lowered his weapon, and went away muttering.

No sooner had he turned his back than one of the demon-women spoke hoarsely to her companions:

"Listen to my dream, women of Lanka. I saw a monkey set fire to the city, and set Ravan on an ass to mock him, and Ravan's heads and arms were hewn off; and Vibishan was made king; and in four days shall this dream come true."

In fear, they bowed to Sita, and hurried from the grove.

Just then, a ring flew through the air, and fell shining at Sita's feet. She picked it up, knew it as Rama's ring, and gave a scream of joy.

"Lady!"

She looked about, and beheld the monkey. She stepped backwards in fear.

"Be not afraid, lady Sita. I am but a monkey, but the noble Rama allows me to call myself his friend. From him I brought the ring, and from him I bring also a message."

He told her all the story.

"In but a few days, lady," he said in closing, "the arrows of Rama will vanquish the demon-king and all his followers, and you will be delivered."

So saying, he left her presence. As he was leaving the grove, he pulled down the branches of an asoka tree, and plucked the fruit and ate. The crackling sound caught the ears of the guards, and they ran to attack the stranger. Hanuman tore up a tree, and swung it round, sweeping the demon soldiers away as a broom might sweep shavings. At length, however, he was seized, and carried away to the court of Ravan, the king. Giant demons and horrid spectres stood in the palace hall, and they feared the very look of the ten-headed lord. But Hanuman had no fear. Ravan burst into a loud laugh when he beheld the monkey.

"Who are you?" he said.

"In me, O King, monkey as I am, you see the messenger of that glorious hero, Rama, who bent and broke the bow of Siva, and whose wife Sita you carried away by brutal force. Be warned, Ravan! I put my hands together, and beg you, be warned ere it is too late, and give back Sita to her Rama."

VIII

"WRETCH!" shouted Ravan. "Dare you address such words to a king?"

Turning to his courtiers, he said:

"Kill the beast."

"Sir," cried Vibishan, his brother, stepping forward and bowing. "That would not be a kingly act. This monkey is a messenger from Rama. He speaks as an ambassador. Kings do not slay ambassadors."

"True," sneered Ravan, the Ten-headed, "but they may take off the ambassadors' tails."

Then Ravan gave the order:

"Tie rags to the creature's tail; steep the rags in oil; set light to them; and when the tail is consumed, let Rama's noble messenger go free."

Hanuman smiled.

Rags were tied on, but there were not enough. More were fetched, and yet more were needed. The fact was, Hanuman's tail was growing by magic. More rags, more oil, more tail! Not a rag was left in the city; every drop of oil was used up! But the demons took no warning from this wonder. Drums were beat and hands were clapped as the tail was set light to.

Suddenly, making his body smaller (but not his tail!) Hanuman slipped out of the grasp of the guards, who held him, and leaped on to the palace roof, his immense tail all in flames.

The palace caught fire. Hanuman leaped to another house, another, another, and so all over the city. A large part of Lanka was in a blaze, but not the house of the good Vibishan, the brother of the king, nor the mansion where Sita was sheltered in the grove of asoka trees. The flames roared.

Springing into the Indian Ocean, the monkey quenched the fiery tail, shortened it by magic to its right length, and hastened to the asoka grove.

"Lady," he said humbly to Sita, "give me a token to carry back to your husband."

She unfastened a shining jewel from her hair and handed it to the loyal messenger.

"Say to my lord," she said, "that he has never yet failed to keep his word, and I wait for him to save me."

He bowed and departed.

Leaping again over the watery channel, he

sprang into the midst of the host of monkeys who awaited him, and they received him with shouts of joy. Again they cheered as they heard the news that Sita was found. The army marched to the Nilghiri mountains, and soon Hanuman was placing the jewel in Rama's hand and telling him the tale of his adventures in Ceylon.

When Rama, his eyes filled with tears of gratitude, put his royal hand on Hanuman's head in blessing, the good soul felt happier than he had ever felt since he was born in the jungle.

"And now," said Rama, "it is the hour for the advance. Call the bears and muster the troops."

Oh! who could count the number of the soldiers in this strange host? In vast regiments they marched—monkeys of many kinds, and bears of many kinds, shaggy and sharp-clawed. Rama, Lakshman, Sugriva, and Hanuman gazed with pride at the mighty host. And so, like a giant river, the living stream of monkeys and bears flowed to the sea.

Meanwhile, fear fell on the breasts of the

demons of Lanka, and they murmured to each other, saying:

"If Rama's messenger who burned our houses is so mighty, what must Rama himself be?"

And word came unto the Queen Mandodari that the people were sore afraid, and she went and fell at the feet of her lord, and said—

"Husband, make no more fight against the Divine Archer, for he will destroy us all, even as the frost destroys a bed of lotuses."

The Raksha laughed with all his ten mouths, and then summoned his council and asked them what he should do.

A dark-faced demon rose and made a speech, and advised war.

Another fierce Raksha said likewise.

Another, with iron teeth, shrieked the same defiance.

Vibishan, the king's brother, spoke in a different tone.

"Pardon my boldness, brother; I beg you to render back Sita to her consort, for the shafts of Rama kill, even as the rays of the sun burn up the grass of the earth."

"Wretch!" howled Ravan, and he rushed

upon Vibishan, and threw him out of the hall of audience.

Then up stood Kumbha-Karna, the king's second brother.

"Ravan," he said solemnly, "you ought never to have taken Sita away. But you are my brother; you are my king. I know my duty, and I will fight at your side till Rama is laid low and Sita his widow becomes your bride."

Vibishan had sprung in one tremendous leap over Adam's bridge and the trembling sea, and jumped down among the astonished bears and monkeys on the shore. He told them who he was, and was led at once to the presence of Rama and Lakshman, and Rama embraced him, and received him as a friend and ally.

Ravan sent spies to spy in the camp of Hanuman, and they were seen and caught. But when their noses and ears were about to be cut off, Rama and Lakshman ran in and spared the captives, and sent them back to Lanka to tell the king all they had seen.

"My lord," said the chief spy, as he knelt at Ravan's feet, "never before was seen such a host of terrible monkeys and bears. I have heard that the number of them is eighteen thousand billions."

A cry of horror went round the court, but Ravan only smiled and sneered.

" Rama is trying to grasp the sky and he will fall with empty hands."

Now was the time come for the army to cross. Rama shot an arrow into the sea, and at this signal a strange figure emerged from the water. It was old Ocean, all shaggy with seaweed and with shells that clung to his body.

" I wish to cross over your realm, sir," said Rama.

" Then, heroic prince, I advise you to give order to the clever monkeys Nala and Nila to construct a causeway over my waves, and I will take care that it shall not be disturbed in any way while you and your followers march to Lanka."

Ocean bowed and retired to his watery palace.

At a word from Rama, Nala and Nila prepared their plan, for they were magical engineers. At another word from Rama the army of bears and monkeys brought the material for the giant bridge, more than thirty miles long. They tore up trees, rocks, and even mountains, and carried them to the master monkeys Nala and Nila.

Soon the work was done. A broad road spanned the sea.

"March," cried the deep voice of Rama.

With a sound as of thunder the troops proceeded across the bridge, and the Divine Archer, seated on a hill, watched the advance of his mighty host. Last of all, Rama and Lakshman rode in their chariot, and ere long they pitched their tent on the shore of Ceylon.

The news of their landing reached the ears of the demon king. But he bade the servants prepare a banquet; and after supper he sat on the throne, his queen at his side, and a royal umbrella over his head, and the dancers danced before him, and the minstrels played the cymbals, drums, and lutes.

It was dusk, and Rama, looking from his tent, saw a flash on the top of the hill of Lanka.

"It lightens," he cried.

"No, sire," observed Vibishan, "that flash was the flash of the crown on Ravan's head, and of the earring in his queen's ear. They are sitting on the thrones and the dancers dance before them."

Rama smiled, and took up his bow, and fitted an arrow, and aimed at the city on the hill, and shot.

The arrow crashed through the umbrella, knocked off the crown, and whisked the gold ring out of the queen's ear! Having done that, the arrow turned in the air and flew back to Rama's quiver.

At this strange event Ravan's ten faces turned pale. He dismissed the players and dancers and courtiers to their homes, and spent the long night arguing with his tearful wife. Over and over again she besought him to yield to Rama.

IX

THE hour had dawned for the assault. Rama's host was divided into four parts for the attack on the four gates of the city of the ten-headed monster.

Roaring and growling, the monkeys and bears, carrying huge masses of rock and timber, and with the war-cry of "Glory to Rama!" rushed upon the fortress.

Demon drums and clarions sounded the alarm, and on the walls appeared swarms of Rakshas flourishing javelins, clubs, maces, axes, picks, swords, bludgeons, bows, arrows, slings, rocks. Horses galloped, elephants charged, chariots rolled. Masses of stone flew through the air. Ravan's palace was reduced to ruins. Night fell, and the two armies rested.

Next day Lakshman headed the attack, and he was met by Meghnad, son of the demon king. Vast masses of earth were flung from side to side, and clouds of dust darkened the air, and in the midst of the hurly-burly Lakshman was engaged in combat with the Lanka prince. Meghnad threw his spear with full force against Lakshman's breast, and the brother of Rama fell in a swoon and was borne from the field. And night fell again. Rama leaned over his beloved brother's form and saw his danger, and sent Hanuman to a far-off mountain where precious herbs of healing grew. In the blackness of the night the faithful monkey hurried to the place of magic plants, culled the herbs, and was back by the bedside of Lakshman before the break of day.

Rama prepared a potion, gave it to his brother, and soon Lakshman arose, gay and refreshed, ready once more for the fray.

Next day the valiant Kumbha-Karna, brother of Ravan, having drunk many jars of wine and eaten many buffaloes, sallied forth to the combat. Showers of rock fell upon him, but he was no more hurt than an elephant by a shower of seeds. Advancing like a moving hill, he caused the bears and monkeys to fly in panic.

And now was the moment for Rama to enter the conflict. He raised his bow, and his arrows rained up, down, right, left, over, under, forwards, straight, slanting, in every possible direction, and at length the terrible Kumbha-Karna lay like a log, and his soul went up to the shining gods, because he was slain by the Divine Archer.

Then flowers fell from the skies, and the kettle-drums rumbled in the clouds, and night fell once more.

Days passed in this tremendous war of Lanka, and time would fail to tell of the deeds of the valiant on either side. Meghnad and many another proud Raksha had fallen, and the last great contest was a duel between the ten-headed king and Rama the glorious.

Each leader stood in his chariot. Now the god Indra had sent down to Rama his golden car, drawn by four flying horses, and also a suit of gleaming armour, and a heavenly sword, and a bow and quiver.

" To-day," shouted Ravan, " I will give you in charge to death, for now you are to meet the all-powerful Ravan."

" Boast not," replied Rama, " but act."

What words can rightly tell of the terror of this battle? Earth and ocean shook as the champions waged their last fight, and the sun turned a dull grey, and the winds ceased to breathe, and the army of Lanka and the host of bears and monkeys stood still and watched, as the darts of Rama flashed, and the twenty hands of the demon wielded awful weapons. And then the arrows were shot from the bow of Indra, and all the world seemed a mass of fire and smoke as the giant form of Ravan fell, and the spirit of the fallen king soared up to the house of Indra and the wondrous gods.

Flowers dropped; kettle-drums rattled in the

upper air; the sun shone golden; and voices from heaven cried:

"Well done, hero, noble and true!"

Queen Mandodari came with her women and made sore lament over the body of the king:

"So thou hast fallen, dear lord, but not by the hand of man; for Rama's strength was divine, and the arrow that slew thee leaped from the bow of Indra. Oh that thou hadst never touched the lady Sita! Oh that thou hadst given ear to my prayer and let her return to her Rama! I remember, beloved one, how, in the days far gone, thou and I were happy in our wedded youth; but the heart of Mandodari will never again know joy."

Rama, the great-souled, showed respect to the fallen foe, and bade that grand funeral rites should be performed. The body of Ravan, richly robed, was laid upon a high pile of sweet-scented wood and covered with many garlands, and the flames flared upwards, and the queen and her women wept, and priests chanted a low and solemn chant for the dead.

Meanwhile Hanuman, the faithful ape, had hastened to the mansion in the grove of asoka trees, and Vibishan went with him; and soon they returned, bearing the fair Princess Sita in a splendid palanquin, and a multitude of guards, staves in hand, marched on either side.

But Rama hurried not to meet her.

And the people wondered.

"Brother," he said to Lakshman, "it is not fitting that my queen should come back to me till, in the sight of all folk, she is proved true to me, her husband. Long time has she dwelt in the home of Ravan, and if her love has wandered from Rama, she cannot stand the test of fire. But if she has always been my faithful spouse, flame will not hurt one lock of her hair. Lakshman, build up the pile."

Lakshman heaped up a stack of wood and set it on fire, and all the people stood by in silence. Then Sita climbed the pile, and for a few moments naught was seen of her form amid the smoke and glow; and the people wept. But the red flames parted, and lo! out of the ordeal of fire, without singe or hurt, the lady Sita stepped down, and the shouts of the army were loud and long as she was clasped in the arms of Rama.

Heavenly flowers fell, and music was heard in

the high air, and the nymphs of cloud-land danced in gay rings.

From the enormous treasure-houses of the demons of Lanka rewards were bestowed upon the army of bears and monkeys, and these sturdy and loyal friends of Rama went homewards, rejoicing that their work was so happily ended.

The good Vibishan took Mandodari to wife, and these two reigned over the beautiful isle of Lanka.

Rama and Sita, Lakshman and Hanuman the faithful monkey, and other comrades in joy and grief, mounted an air chariot drawn by flying swans and soared upwards on the journey to Ayodhya city. And as they sailed peacefully through the air they looked down upon the scenes of earth.

They saw the isle of Ceylon as a gem in the ocean—the bridge of Rama that joined the island to the shore of India—the land of the monkeys and the bears and Sugriva their king—the rocky Nilghiri hills—the wood where the golden deer was slain and Ravan snatched Sita from her husband's care—the stream of Godaveri in the jungle where Lakshman built the bamboo hut—the forest-home of Saint Agastya—the hill of Chitra-Kuta—the retreat of the white-haired hermit Valmiki—the sacred river of Ganges. Had not the holy river promised Sita that she should safely cross his waves again? And the word had come true.

A winged genie had carried the news of Rama's coming to the Prince Bharat in Ayodhya. Crowds filled the streets and gardens, and spread along the city walls. Flags waved. Festoons were gay. Troops marched to music. Priests chanted. Heralds shouted proclamations. Dancers leaped. Elephants trumpeted. Drums rolled.

The swan-car descended.

Prince Bharat bowed before his brother, and laid at his feet the pair of sandals which had rested on the throne ever since Rama had left the palace fourteen years before; and the brothers embraced. And Rama's mother, Kausalya, clasped his neck and shed tears of gladness.

The whole city shook with cheers.

Flowers floated from the skies.

The kettle-drums of the gods rumbled.

X

But alas! it was not many days ere evil tongues set going a murmur in the streets and the busy bazaars.

"Is it right," the murmuring voices said, "that queen Sita, having lived in the house of Ravan, the Demon King of Lanka, should now again take her place at the side of her royal lord Rama?"

"It is not right," answered other voices.

Rama gave way to the will of the people. He sent his wife Sita out of his palace, to dwell in the forest in a new exile. Oh that he had shut his ears to false words! Oh that he had held fast to his faith in Sita, and let no evil shadow come between them.

Rama was a good and noble prince, and he ruled justly over the city and land of Ayodhya; but he was alone, and his spirit was often weary.

Where was Sita?

She found shelter in the hut of the aged Saint Valmiki. Under that shelter she became the mother of twin boys. She named them Lava and Kusa. Years would pass before these children would look upon the face of their father Rama.

But that day came in this wise.

Rama said to his brother Lakshman:

"It is time to prove my power over all the chiefs and kings of this region. Take a black horse, therefore, and let it roam where it will, from place to place; and if any king dares to lay hands upon it, make war upon him in my name. And so make a circuit of all the lands round about, and when all is finished the horse shall be sacrificed to the gods, and there shall be a feast."

And it came to pass that after this was done, and no king had stood up against the power of Rama, the black steed was slain by the knives of Brahmans, and its flesh was burned, and word was carried far and near to all folk, high and low, prince and peasant and priest, to attend the feast and the giving of gifts. So people came as flies to the honey, and countless was the host of nobles and knights, beggars and widows and orphans, that gathered at the sacrifice of the horse, and received presents of all kinds from the bounty of Rama.

Now, among the guests that came to the feast

was the old hermit Valmiki, and he brought with him two dark-eyed, handsome lads. He had reared them in the way of the simple life, water from the forest spring for their drink, and berries and fruits for food. Much learning had he taught these sons of Sita—for they were Lava and Kusa—and they could recite thousands of verses that told the tale of Rama's life and deeds.

To the assembled princes and people the lads spoke from memory the *Ramayana*—the poem of Rama; and the ears of the folk were charmed by the music of the harps and the sweet verses of the song.

Rama wished to give them a fee of many gold pieces, but they would take naught.

"Who taught you this poem?" he asked.

"Saint Valmiki taught us; and if it be your pleasure, sir, we will come again and sing more."

That evening they returned to their mother and the aged hermit in the forest.

Next day the crowds sat and listened with delight to more of the song. And so, day by day, the grand chant of the *Ramayana* was chanted by the young harpers of the woods.

And day by day the people noticed the wondrous likeness between the lads and the King of Ayodhya; and day by day Rama himself felt the sense of kinship grow within his breast, till at last he asked old Valmiki many questions concerning the birth of the boys, and then at length learned that they were his own sons, and he pressed them to his breast and bade them stay with him in his house. . . .

But where was Sita?

Rama's heart was sore smit with remorse. He was ashamed to think how he had yielded to the murmurs of the city. Had not Sita passed through the fire in Lanka, and had not hundreds of thousands of his followers beheld how she came out of the flames, unhurt, and had he not taken her to himself in peace and trust and love?

Was Sita yet alive?

Yes; so the hermit said.

And where did she hide her sorrows?

In the hut of old Valmiki in the jungle.

"Father," said Rama, "does Sita still cherish affection for me after all I have done?"

"She holds you in her remembrance as dear as ever," answered Valmiki.

"And will you tell her I repent me of my folly, and that I long—oh, ever so much—to see her and have her in my home again?"

"I will bring her to you to-morrow morning," said the saint.

A great concourse of people were got together the next day, and they and Rama and his sons, Lava and Kusa, waited for the coming of the lady Sita.

She came.

Pale her face, and thin her frame, after the much suffering of her life of exile.

The light of the old love was in her eyes as she approached the royal house.

But she never more entered it.

She saw her husband on the throne. She saw the multitudes of citizens. She saw the splendid crowd of princes and nobles that had come to the feast of the sacrifice of the horse. And above all these she saw the faces of angels, and nymphs of the sky, and the shining gods.

Then Sita cast down her eyes to the ground, and said:

"O mother earth, am I not thy daughter?

Dost thou not know me and all that I have ever done in my life? Thou knowest, mother, that I have been a good and true wife to Rama. Thou knowest how I have laboured for him and for our children. Thou knowest the pain of my soul all these many years. And now, mother, let my sorrows have an end. Take me to thy rest!"

And when she had said these words, behold! the earth opened, and there rose out of it a throne of gold, and the throne was surrounded by glorious spirits that shone with bright jewels. And the lady Sita cast one look of love at her husband and her sons, and all the folk around, and she sat upon the throne, and she and her earth-spirits sank from view, and the ground closed over her head, and Sita was gone for ever to the great mother in the under-world.

And Rama was in his house alone.

Note.—The foregoing tale is based on two versions of the national Indian legend—(1) *The Ramayana of Tulsi Das*, translated from the Hindi by F. S. Growse, published at Cawnpore in 1891; (2) *Ramayana, the Epic of Rama, Prince of India*, condensed into English verse by Romesh Dutt, published by Messrs. Dent, and obtainable in cheap form. Mr. Dutt's work is founded on the oldest version, namely, the Sanskrit; and this differs in various particulars from that of Tulsi Das.

Speaking of the influence of this story on the popular mind, Mr. Dutt says: "The *Ramayana* is still a living tradition and a living faith. It forms the basis of the moral instruction of a nation, and it is a part of the lives of two hundred millions of people."

The original poem is of very great length, and is interspersed with moral and religious reflections, which have been omitted in the preceding story of "The Divine Archer." In the belief of the mass of the Indian people, Rama is a god in human shape.

THE FIVE PRINCES

THE FIVE PRINCES

FIVE princes, brothers, wandered in a forest. They were the sons of an Indian king. Now this king had two wives, Koontee and Madree, and the young men were sons to one or the other of the queens. The two sons of Madree were thus half-brothers to the three sons of Koontee.

A hard fate drove them from their home-land. For thirteen years they must not see their country. For thirteen years they must be exiles. They must hide from their foes.

A dread place was the wood where they hid. Tall trees put out their great arms and made a black shade. The thin-legged deer ran to and fro in the glades. Bears stole in and out of the bushes. Snakes lurked in nooks. Wild bees hummed. Birds of strange shape flew from tree to tree.

The five princes, two sons of Madree, three sons of Koontee, felt a deep thirst, and nowhere could they see the sweet shine of water.

Then Yudhisthira, who was more than a

prince—he was a king—said to his half-brother Nakula:

"O Nakula, son of Madree, climb yonder tree and look all ways, and see if water is near; look if any plants that grow in moist soil are in this jungle, for they will be a sign of water."

Then Nakula, who was the twin-brother to Sahadev, went up the tree as he was bid, and he looked this way and that, and he made a shout:

"Yes, I can see plants and leaves that live in the damp. And hark! I can hear the sharp call of the cranes."

Said the king:

"Make haste down, Nakula. Take your arrow-case with you and fill it with water at the pool or spring where the cranes are, and bring your brothers a precious draught!"

So Nakula came down with speed, and he ran with his quiver in hand to the place where he had caught sight of the green plants. A smooth, clear pool was there, and on the edge of it he beheld cranes, birds with long legs and long necks; their tails feathery, their eyes eager and watchful; and a red tuft was on each head. The cranes snapped at worms, at small snakes, at frogs, at fish, and now and then tore up a weed from the pool.

But the prince had no care for cranes. He was all but mad with thirst. Down on his knees he fell. He leaned his head to the clear pool.

"Stay!" cried a voice. "Stay, young man! Drink naught till you have done as the law of this pool bids. None may drink here till he has made answer to the questions I ask. Answer first, and then fill your quiver."

Nakula paid no heed. He drank. The next moment he fell dead among the reeds that grew at the brink of the water.

The cranes waded in the pool. Wild bees hummed. Deer trotted through the jungle. The dead prince held the quiver in his hand; and his four brothers waited.

Finding that he did not return, the king said: "Sahadev, we will not wait longer. I know not why your brother delays. Go and fetch water for us, for we are faint, and can scarce move. Follow the track your brother went."

When Sahadev reached the water he saw the dead youth, and his heart was sore troubled; yet was his thirst so great that he had no will to stay and weep over his lost one, and he knelt to drink.

"Halt," cried a loud voice. "Do not take one drop of this water until you have made reply to my questions; else it will mean death!"

The prince said not a word. He bent over the pool, and then rolled upon the earth dead.

Side by side lay the brothers—the twin sons of Madree the queen. And the bear of the woods crept among the bushes in search of berries, and the gleam of the tiger's eyes was bright in the jungle.

Two brothers dead; three brothers living; and dry were the mouths of the three.

Said the king:

"Have you strength, Arjuna, brother of mine, to go to the pool and fetch water? Your brother and I are weak with thirst. Oh, haste, Arjuna, haste!"

When Arjuna saw his two dead brothers he put his arrow to the bow and looked about for the foe that had slain them, so that he might slay the slayer. But he saw no living man. Then the thirst came so strong upon him that he must drink; so he stooped down.

"Beware," cried a voice. "Drink not until

you have answered my questions. To drink now will be your doom."

"Who are you, vile man?" shouted Arjuna; and he shot one arrow this way among the reeds, and another among the trees; and he pulled out darts from his bundle, and flung them up, and north and south, and east and west; but he saw no man.

"Ha, ha, ha," laughed the voice. "You cannot strike me, prince. Answer, if you wish to live."

Arjuna knelt and was about to drink. He also fell dead.

"Alas!" sighed the king, "they come not back. What can have happened? Perhaps they are all too faint to walk. Will you, dear Bhima, go for drink?"

Then Bhima rose slowly and crept to the pool, and he was in great sorrow when he saw the three dead youths; but he was so parched that he could not stay to mourn.

"Drink not," said the voice. "Let not water touch your lips till you have given answer to my questions; else you will breathe your last!"

And Bhima also died.

Silent was the forest, except for the murmur of bees and the sounds of bird and beast; and the king sat in pain of thirst. At last he arose, and with slow steps he wended his way to the pool.

Loud was his wail when he saw the four dead men, and he glanced all round to see who it was that smote them, but he could discover no enemy. And then he bent towards the water where grew the lilies.

"Stay!" cried the voice. "Unless you answer my questions ere you drink, death will fall upon you; such is the law of this place. I, the old crane with the red crest, rule over the pool, and I dare you to drink."

"No crane," replied the king, "would have such power. You must be some bad genie. Show yourself!"

He saw the crane amid the reeds.

"King," said the bird, "I am indeed a genie. But hearken unto my warning. Drink not yet."

"Repeat your questions."

"How can a man become wise?"

"By learning the sacred texts of the hymns—the blessed *Vedas*."

"Who is he that is not rich, though he looks well and fair?"

"The man who has much and gives naught."

"What is heavier than the world and higher than the clouds?"

"The love of father and mother."

"Whose eyes never close?"

"The fish's eyes."

"Which is the way to be happy?"

"To say truth and be kind."

"How may a man be a true Brahman?"

"Not by saying texts from the holy scriptures; not by praying many prayers; but by just deeds and right life."

These and other questions did the king answer.

Then said the spirit of the pool:

"Well have you spoken. Drink."

Then said the spirit of the pool again:

"Well pleased am I with your speech, and now I give you a boon. You may name which you will of these dead men, and he whom you choose shall live."

There was silence. Said the king:

"I will choose Nakula, son of Madree."

"But he is only your half-brother. Will you not choose your own brother, Bhima, or your own brother, Arjuna? Did you not love them?"

"Yea, I loved them," said the king. "But I wish that Nakula should come back to life."

"Why?"

"Because he is the son of Madree, and I am the son of Koontee. Now, after the thirteen years of wandering, we shall return to our home, and the two queens will come forth to see us. Two only of the five brethren will they see. And if Madree sees that both are the sons of Koontee, and she learns that her twin sons are dead, then will her heart faint and be like to break. Therefore, O spirit, let us be just to the mother's heart, and let one son of each mother bring gladness to their eyes."

The crane was no more seen. But as it fled away its voice was heard saying softly:

"Noble-hearted prince! You have chosen Nakula before your own dearest brothers, and you wished to be just rather than snatch at what would best please your own soul. Therefore they all shall live!"

And the four brothers rose up.

Note.—The story is adapted from the beautiful version, entitled "The Enchanted Lake," in Sir Edwin Arnold's *Indian Idylls*. The original tale is in the Indian epic, *The Mahabharata*.

WHAT LOVE CAN DO

WHAT LOVE CAN DO

" The love that moves the sun and all the stars."—*Dante.*

Now, there was a king in India whose name was Aswapati (As-wa-pah-tee), and the folk loved him, and he gave help to all in need, and he served the shining gods in prayer and sacrifice.

But he had no son or daughter in whom his name and line could live on, when the time came for him to die, and his heart was grieved, and he fasted oft, and said hymns to the shining gods, and burned offerings on their holy altar, and hoped they would grant him the gift he asked. When sixteen years had thus passed, his prayer was heard. In the red fire of the altar he beheld a lady of fair look and ways, and she said to him:

" Thy faith hath pleased me, O Raja, and if thou wilt say thy desire, it shall be given thee."

" Goddess," replied the king, " my wish is to have a child to live after me."

"The Lord of heaven," she said, "will grant thee what thou hast prayed."

She was gone, and the Raja saw only the red flame.

A babe was born—a girl, with bright eyes, bright like the lotus lily, as the Indian people say—and she was the glory of her mother and father. She grew to be so sweet a maid that her father made sure that kings would come from far and near to seek her as a wife. But none came, for she—the lotus-eyed—had a soul that seemed too great for even kings, and her serious ways and speech kept men in awe.

Now, one day, this maid of grace—Savitri (Sah-vee-tree) by name—had knelt at the altar of Agni, god of the red flame, and had laid there an offering of cakes and drink. Then she took up a bunch of flowers in the holy place, and came and gave them to her sire, Aswapati. He gazed upon her with tender eyes and said:

"Daughter, it is time you should be wed after the manner of high-born ladies, lest folk should think that I am at fault in not choosing a husband for you. And since no man comes to pay suit to you, I pray you go where you will and choose for yourself."

So she bowed herself before her sire, and took her leave, and rode in a splendid car along with elders and wise men, whom the king had told to go with her up and down the land. The car passed through forests and along the streets of great towns, and among the hamlets of the hills, and wherever she went the princess gave alms to the poor and greetings to high and low, and the people blessed her.

At last she came back and the Raja was on his throne, and the wise man, Narad, sat at his side.

"Father," she said, "I have done as you bade, and I have found my choice. It is the Prince Satyavan. Prince he is, yet he dwells not in a royal house."

"Wherefore?" asked the Raja.

"He has no kingdom, and lives in a cottage in the woods with his father and mother. A noble pair are they, but sad is their lot. The old man is blind, and he and his queen have had their home many years, ever since their son was a babe, in this jungle, for enemies drove them from their kingdom, and took from the king his rightful throne. My prince is noble, and his name shows what he is, for at his birth the Brahmans called him Truth-lover. Gay and strong is he, and a rider of horses, and his hand has a gift for painting horses in pictures that are a wonder to see."

"What think you?" asked the king of Narad, the wise.

"Alas!" answered Narad, "Ill has she chosen. The old king indeed is a just man, and the Prince Satyavan is a noble youth, but there is a dark fate that waits for him, for it has been shown to me by the shining gods that in a year from this very day he shall die."

"Hear you that, my daughter?" cried the king. "O choose some other, choose some other, for the Lord of Death, even Yama, will come in a year and claim your husband for his own. Choose some other."

"I can choose none other, father dear," said the maid. "To Satyavan alone is my heart given, and though Death will take him in a year, yet him only will I wed."

"Let it be so, child," sighed the Raja.

"Strange will your bridal be. You will have your home in the wilderness, and in twelve months be left a mourner."

The king and his courtiers and priests set forth to the woods, carrying with them much treasure, and they found the blind old king seated on a grass mat beneath a sal tree.

"Be seated, sir!" said the blind Raja, when he knew that a king had come to see him.

So Aswapati sat on the grass mat, and the blind king offered him water from a jar, for he was poor, and had neither wine nor silver cups. And the two kings agreed upon the marriage, and soon the prince and the maid were wed in the forest, and when she was made lady of the little cot among the trees of the jungle, her sire kissed her with many tears, and her friends said farewells, and they departed. As soon as they were gone, she took off her jewels and sparkling dress, and she put on a plain robe made of bark of trees, and a cloak of yellow cloth. Her queenhood was not in her jewels or her dress, but in her kind soul and the sweet service she did to the blind old king and his wife, and in the love she bore to the prince of her choice.

So passed the happy year, and only four days more would go by ere the Shadow of Death would glide into the forest kingdom of her lord, and take him from her arms. For three days she fasted and she had no sleep, and her heart was in pain at the dread of that which was to come. But Satyavan, the noble prince, knew naught of the fate that waited for his life.

On the morning of the last day rose Satyavan, in blithe mood, and he took his woodman's axe for felling trees, and said, smiling:

" Dear wife, I go forth to hew down trees, and at set of sun, I shall be home again."

Her heart smote her at the words, for she knew that the black-robed Yama would lay his thin hand upon her love and take him hence.

" I will go with you this day," she said.

" Nay," he cried, " the ground is rough for your feet, and the way will be long, and you will be faint."

" Let me go, Satyavan," begged the princess in the robe of bark.

He said her nay no more, and they walked to the distant spot where grew the trees he meant to fell, and the wild fruit that she would gather in her basket.

The hour of noon had passed, and the dusk was creeping upon the great forest. The sound of the axe echoed in the grove. Basket in hand, Savitri plucked ripe berries from the shrubs, but often and often she paused and she looked at the wood-cutter, and she looked again. . . .

"Oh, wife," he called.

She ran to his side, and set her basket down.

"My head, my head! A pang shoots sharp through my brain. Hot is my blood. I must lie down."

She sat beneath a tree and laid his head upon her lap, and fanned his face. His eyes were closed, his pulse was slow, and now it was still.

The year had flown.

Before her stood a tall shadow that had the shape of a man, and its robe was black, and a red light was in its eyes, and a crown was on its head.

"Are you one of the holy gods?" she asked in a low voice.

"Lady," it said, "I am Yama, the Lord of Death, and I am come for the prince you love."

He lifted his hand, and in it was a cord, and he flung the cord, and lo! it caught the life of the prince in its noose, and drew it from his bosom, and Satyavan was dead, and Death turned its face towards the south, for the south (so the Indian fables tell) was its kingdom.

Dark was the jungle.

Strong was Death.

But the woman was brave.

She rose up and followed in the steps of Death.

Presently, the black god, hearing her footsteps, turned and spoke:

"Go back. You have come far from home. Go back, and do those sad rites in which mourners show their sorrow for the dead."

"I must go," she replied, "where my husband goes. That is my duty. The wise men say that to walk seven steps with another makes them friends. So let me walk more than seven steps with you. And the wise men also say that the best road to walk is that of right."

"Well have you convinced me," said the Lord of Death, "and in return for the good words, I promise that, except the soul of Satyavan, I will give you what you will."

"Then give me a gift for my prince's father, and let the eyes of the old king once more behold the light of day, and let his strength be as the strength of the sun."

"It shall be done," said Death; "but now you must turn back, for you have far to go; and my way leads only to Doom."

"I shall never be weary of the way that my husband goes. There is no sweeter fruit on earth than the company of those we love."

The black god smiled, for her words were good and precious.

"Once again, I will give you a gift, except the soul of Satyavan."

"Thanks again, O Death; and now I will ask that the kingdom of the old Raja shall be restored to him, so that he may have his land as well as his sight."

"Lady, it shall happen as you wish. And

now, go back. The forest is wide, and home is distant."

"Master of Death, hear me once more. What is the goodness of the good man? Is it kindness to all things in earth, air, or sea? It is indeed, and even if an enemy seeks help, the good man will be ready to grant him aid."

"Fair is your saying, princess; and for these blessed words I will promise yet another boon. Speak."

"O Death, I would be mother to noble children, and teach them to walk in the steps of their dear father, Satyavan. Give me my prince."

Then Yama, King of Death, shook the cord that he held in his hand.

"Lady, your husband shall reign long years with you, and your sons shall reign after you."

The dark shade that wore the crown had floated into the gloom of the jungle.

With quick feet she ran. Breathless, she flew. And when she reached the tree under which the body of Satyavan lay, she knelt, she placed the head on her lap, she watched; and the eyes opened, and the lips said:

"I have slept a long time. Just as I was falling into slumber, I seemed to see a vision of a shadow that seized my very life in a magic noose, and bore it away I know not where."

"It was Yama, Lord of Death. But he is not here. Rise, Satyavan, for it is night, and we must go home."

"Ah!" he said, "now I call to mind that a sharp pang shot through my brow."

"To-morrow let us talk of what has happened to-day. Let us go."

"The night is dark. We could not find the path."

"Look!" she said, "some way off a fire has been burning to-day in the forest—the work of the blazing sun at mid-day, perhaps. I will fetch a brand, and we will wave it as we walk, so as to scare away the beasts of the jungle. Or, if you will, let us stay here till your pain is all gone."

"It has gone, Savitri. I am strong again. My father and mother will grieve at our absence."

As he thought of his blind father (ah! but was he blind now?) the prince's eyes filled with tears.

So he sprang to his feet, and brushed off the dry leaves that clung to his clothes.

"There is your basket of fruit," he cried.

"Fetch it to-morrow, Satyavan. We have enough to do to find our way in the dark. But I will carry the axe."

She carried the axe in her left hand, and her right arm was about his waist; and his left arm was about her neck; and so they wended their way through the jungle; nor did bear or tiger harm them.

The sky was becoming grey when they reached the hamlet where the old king and queen and their few companions lived. They heard voices crying eagerly. A shout arose when the prince and princess were seen.

"My children!" cried the king.

"Father!" exclaimed Satyavan. "How is this? You were able to see me?"

"My son, my eyes can see once more. I know not how the marvel came about, but I do know I can see my son. And you, dear Savitri, for the first time can I now look upon my faithful daughter!"

After he had held them some moments, and gazed at them both with joy, he asked:

"And where have you been all the night? Tell me, Satyavan, what kept you so long?"

"Father," said Savitri, "he does not know all that took place in the night. Let me tell the tale."

So they sat down — king, queen, prince, princess, and their comrades and loyal friends, and the soft voice of Savitri told:—

How they wandered in the forest;

How the curse had been foretold by Narad, the sage, and how it must be fulfilled at the end of the year;

How Satyavan died;

How Death came;

And how she had followed Death and what had been said.

Now, while the king and his friends thus listened, and their hearts were moved by the story, a great noise was heard in the forest. Along the glade they saw a crowd of people approach—soldiers, officers, citizens.

"News, good news!" the people cried. "The tyrant who took the throne by unjust means and cruel power has been overthrown. Come back to us, dear king. Blind though you are, you shall at least know that we gather round you in true service."

"Thanks be to the shining gods, my people," said the old king, "I can see you all; and I will go with you, and see my kingdom once again."

Note.—The story is based on Sir Edwin Arnold's poem "Savitri, or Love and Death," in his *Indian Idylls:* also on the version of the same episode in Mr. Romesh Chunder Dutt's translation of the *Mahabharata*.